The Perfect Wedding Planner

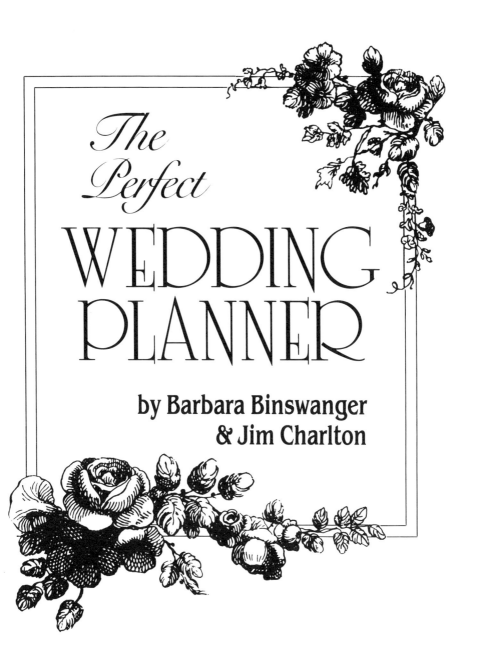

The *Perfect* WEDDING PLANNER

by Barbara Binswanger
& Jim Charlton

DELACORTE PRESS

Published by
Delacorte Press
Bantam Doubleday Dell Publishing Group, Inc.
666 Fifth Avenue
New York, New York 10103

Library of Congress Cataloging in Publication Data

Binswanger, Barbara.
The perfect wedding planner / Barbara Binswanger and Jim
Charlton.
p. cm.
ISBN 0-385-30080-8 (hc) : $14.95
1. Weddings—United States—Planning—Handbooks, manuals, etc.
I. Charlton, James, 1939— . II. Title.
HQ745.B63   1990
395'.22—dc20   90-3768
                                                   CIP
Manufactured in the United States of America
Published simultaneously in Canada

January 1991

10 9 8 7 6 5 4 3 2 1
KPP

Contents

The Perfect Wedding Planner

*Y*our wedding is the most exciting and complicated party you will ever give. Like any big event, it takes planning, organization, and attention to detail. But how do you make intelligent, thoughtful decisions at a highly emotional time like this? More importantly, how do you remember the decisions you've made? Well, relax. You've already made one decision that will make all the others easier. You have a copy of *The Perfect Wedding Planner*.

The Perfect Wedding Planner grew out of our experiences planning our own wedding. It's based on the notebook that Barbara's mother developed to keep track of all those names, telephone numbers, estimates, and reservations that have a way of disappearing when they are just written down on scraps of paper. Ideally, every couple should have Barbara's mother or an experienced consultant plan their wedding, but *The Perfect Wedding Planner* is the next best thing!

The three-ring binder format makes this the most personal, most flexible, and most useful planner available. If you need more pages for any section—the guest list, for example—simply photocopy and add as many as necessary. Add dividers, pockets, blank pages for notes—whatever makes it work best for you. *The Perfect Wedding Planner* is, first and foremost, a workbook.

Though it is filled with suggestions to make planning easier, it is not designed to take the place of an etiquette book. There are a number of good ones available in your bookstore or library. We won't tell you how to word your invitations or where to seat divorced parents, but we do give you pages to get estimates from stationers and space to plan out your seating arrangements. So forget every compunction you ever had about writing in books and grab your pencil. Fill in names, dates, descriptions, and prices. We've included a page for everything, so you won't forget anything!

We recommend that you read the entire book through once carefully to get a sense of the scope of the arrangements that can be made. It won't take long. If your time is short or your wedding less formal, some aspects may not be important to you. We didn't use at-home cards or announcements, for instance, but they are included here in case your situation calls for them. Just use what makes sense to you and then adapt or forget the rest. The calendar/checklist on pages 3–5 will give you a good idea of the order in which decisions should be made; use it to figure out your top priorities.

As you will see, the fill-in pages are self-explanatory and will guide you through every planning phase. But there are a few tips that will be important in every selection process and it is worth stating them now.

Every time you make a phone call, get the name of the person who helps you and write it down in the space provided. This is absolutely essential. Dealing with the same person each time insures that she will be familiar with your wedding and the services you will need as well as the prices she has quoted you.

Be forthright about your budget. If you plan to spend between $200 and $400 on a wedding gown, say so immediately. Don't waste everyone's time by trying on gowns you can't possibly afford. The same goes for every other supplier, from the caterer to the florist. Professionals should be able to handle any budget creatively and enthusiastically. If they don't feel that way, you are better off without them.

Ask questions. Find out exactly what services are provided and at what cost. And get everything in writing! Are delivery dates specified? Are deposits refundable? Will the cake be delivered, or must someone pick it up? Read that fine print! Does the orchestra contract specify which musicians will be playing or just list a band name? One couple we know hired a band for their wedding after hearing the group perform. When the band showed up it was a different group performing under the same name. The wedding party was disappointed, but they had no recourse.

Talk to your friends. The experience of another couple we know caused us to have a little talk with our photographer. We didn't want him yelling out "Smile" during our recessional, as theirs did! And it was a friend of Barbara's mother's who put us on to the baroque musicians we used, and another who suggested the trick that enabled us to use the same hotel room for both the ceremony and seated buffet reception. Remember, too, that bridal magazines are great reference sources, with information on everything from wedding dresses to honeymoon plans.

Do try to relax as much as possible. With *The Perfect Wedding Planner* you have the details well in hand, and that should ease everyone's mind. The time spent planning your wedding—be it one week or six months—is exciting and wonderful. Enjoy!

CHAPTER 1

The Bride's Checklist and Calendar

*U*se this checklist to plan the perfect wedding! Remember, this is an ideal timetable. If your schedule is too tight or your wedding less formal, adapt and compress it to suit your own style. The starred items apply to every wedding, even an elopement, and each item is dealt with in greater detail throughout the book. The calendar that follows the checklist will help you schedule the myriad appointments and parties leading up to your wedding day.

AS SOON AS POSSIBLE

✓Select a wedding date and time, ideally three to six months beforehand.*

✓Call clergyman or other official to confirm date and schedule appointment to discuss ceremony.

✓Agree on size and degree of formality of wedding.

✓Discuss budget and how expenses will be shared.

✓Book site for the ceremony.

✓Book site for the reception.

✓Begin drawing up your guest list. Inform groom's family of the number they can invite and the date by which you need their list.

✓Send engagement announcement to newspapers, if you wish to.

Begin making honeymoon plans, if you will take one.

THREE MONTHS AHEAD

✓Order invitations and announcements, if needed.

✓Order personal stationery and monogrammed favors for reception.

✓ Choose wedding attendants. Find out their sizes.

✓Order bridal gown; schedule fittings and delivery date.

3

✓Choose a caterer and plan menu.

✓Engage a florist and discuss color scheme and style of wedding.

Audition and/or select music/musicians for ceremony.

✓Audition and/or select music/musicians for reception.

✓Select a wedding photographer.

Select a videographer.

Schedule appointment for bridal portrait.

✓Order attendants' gowns and schedule fittings and delivery.

Select china, crystal, and silver patterns and register gift choices.

TWO MONTHS AHEAD

✓Select a bakery and order wedding cake.

✓Select style of formalwear for groom's party and make arrangements with rental shop.

✓Order any rental equipment necessary—tables, chairs, etc.—for ceremony or reception.

Inform attendants of fitting schedules and of any accessories they may need to buy.

Address invitations and announcements.

Begin making transportation and accommodation arrangements for out-of-town guests and the wedding party.

Begin personal shopping for clothes needed for prewedding parties or honeymoon.

Make any necessary personal appointments—legal, medical, beauty.

Check into health and home insurance needs for after the wedding.

Arrange a floater insurance policy to cover wedding gifts while they are in your parents' home.

Make a gift record and begin writing thank-you notes as gifts arrive.

ONE MONTH AHEAD

Mail invitations.

Check with wedding professionals:

☐ Caterer	☐ Videographer
☐ Florist	☐ Musicians
☐ Photographer	☐ Hotel/Club Manager

✓Buy wedding rings.

Investigate requirements/get blood tests and marriage license.*
Schedule wedding rehearsal and notify everyone involved.
Make necessary changes if you plan to take your husband's name.
Make certain you have all necessary accessories for your wedding gown.
Finish personal shopping.
Finalize honeymoon plans.
Confirm plans with hosts of rehearsal dinner and other parties.
Plan bridesmaids' luncheon.
Buy bridesmaids' and other special gifts.

ONE TO TWO WEEKS AHEAD

Arrange for final fitting and delivery of all wedding attire.
Confirm final guest count and inform:

    ☐ Caterer   ☐ Bakery

    ☐ Hotel/Club Manager

Have final consultation with:

    ☐ Florist   ☐ Videographer

    ☐ Photographer   ☐ Musicians

Send wedding announcements to newspapers.
Finalize transportation and accommodation arrangements for out-of-town guests and wedding party.
Have blood tests and apply for marriage license, if you have not done so.*
Pack an "emergency kit" with safety pins, tissues, cosmetics, needle and thread, and extra lingerie to take to the ceremony site.
Arrange reception seating.
Make certain you have all necessary papers—tickets, passport, traveler's checks, etc.—for your honeymoon, and confirm reservations.
Pack for honeymoon.
Keep writing thank-you notes!
Relax whenever possible!

A SIX-MONTH CALENDAR

Use a current calendar to fill in the following pages accurately. The first month of this personal calendar should be the sixth month before your wedding, so if you are planning to be a June bride, make the first month January.

January

SUNDAY	MONDAY	TUESDAY	WEDNESDAY	THURSDAY	FRIDAY	SATURDAY
		1	2	3	4	5
6	7	8	9	10	11	12
13	14	15	16	17 Country Club 5:30	18	19
20	21	22 Engagement photos Frank King 7:30	23 Mom & Dress shopping Reh. Party 3:45	24 Mom & I bought dress - Pat Marquits	25 Dale & I picked Tuxes Formal Affairs found dress	26 Michele & I Shopping - found dress
27 Mom, Dale & me Linda's Cake Shop 1:30	28 Attendants fitting 4:300	29 Ladybug fittings 3:00	30	31		

February

SUNDAY	MONDAY	TUESDAY	WEDNESDAY	THURSDAY	FRIDAY	SATURDAY
					1	2 Love Winter - East Berlin
3	4	5	6	7	8	9
10	11	12	13	14	15	16
17	18	19	20 Rev. Perry 4:15	21 Album fitting 6:00	22	23
24	25	26	27 $78 due on cake	28		

March

SUNDAY	MONDAY	TUESDAY	WEDNESDAY	THURSDAY	FRIDAY	SATURDAY
					1	2
3	4	5	6	7	8	9
10	11	12	13	14	15	16
17 OK to get marriage license	18	19	20	21	22	23
24	25	26	27	28	29	30
31						

April

SUNDAY	MONDAY	TUESDAY	WEDNESDAY	THURSDAY	FRIDAY	SATURDAY
	1	2	3	4	5	6
7	8	9	10	11	12	13
14	15	16	17	18	19	20
21	22	23	24	25	26	27 Cal of cake due – 777
28	29	30				

May

SUNDAY	MONDAY	TUESDAY	WEDNESDAY	THURSDAY	FRIDAY	SATURDAY
			1	2	3 — Have Bulletins at church by today	4
5	6	7	8	9 — Dale + Mor. Final fitting	10 — Rehearsal 7 pm	11
12	13	14	15	16	17	18
19	20	21	22	23	24	25
26	27	28	29	30	31	

SUNDAY	MONDAY	TUESDAY	WEDNESDAY	THURSDAY	FRIDAY	SATURDAY

CHAPTER 2

Planning the Wedding Budget

TRADITIONAL BREAKDOWN OF EXPENSES
FOR THE BRIDE AND BRIDE'S FAMILY

All reception costs, including room rental, food, and beverages.

Bridesmaids' bouquets and flowers for ceremony and reception.

Any other decorative accessories for ceremony or reception.

Musicians for both ceremony and reception.

Groom's wedding gift and wedding band.

Bridesmaids' gifts. Housing for bridesmaids.

Wedding photographs. Wedding stationery.

Bride's wedding gown, accessories, and trousseau.

All transportation and parking expenses for ceremony and reception.

Bride's blood test and physical.

FOR THE GROOM AND GROOM'S FAMILY

Bride's rings and wedding gift.

Marriage license.

Gifts for the groom's party.

Ties and gloves for the groom's party.

Bride's bouquet and corsage.

Corsages for mothers and grandmothers.

Boutonnieres for groom's party.

Clergyman's fee.

Groom's blood test.

Rehearsal dinner.

The wedding trip.

The Wedding Budget

ITEM	PROJECTED COST	ACTUAL COST

WEDDING GOWN

Dress/Veil _554.00 125.00_ — $ 752.14

Accessories _Slip. 32.40   Bra 30.00_ — 62.40

Total _____ — $ 814.54

WEDDING RINGS

Bride's _____ — 1700.00

Groom's _____ — 200.00

Total _____ — 1900.00

STATIONERY

Invitations _____ — 106.00

Announcements _____ — _____

Informal Note Cards _____ — _____

At-Home Cards _____ — _____

Reception Favors _____ — _____

Calligraphy/Hand-Addressing _____ — _____

Postage _____ — 35.00 approx.

Total _____ — _____

CATERER

Food _____ — _____

Liquor/Beverages _____ — _____

Wedding Cake _____ — 185.—

Other Services _lighted trees_ — 150.—

Total _____ — _____

FLORIST

Ceremony Site _____   _____

Bouquets _____   _____

Corsages/Boutonnieres_____   _____350.00_ approx.

Wedding Cake, Table, Knife _185.-_____   _____185.00_____

Reception Site _____   _____

Other Services _____   _____

     Total _____ $ 535.00

PHOTOGRAPHER
album
~~Formal Portraits~~_____   _____145.00_____

Wedding Package _____   _____700.00_____

     Total _____ $ 845.00

VIDEOGRAPHER

Wedding Package _____   _____

Copies _____   _____

     Total _____   _____

FEES

Ceremony Site _75,-_____ $ 75.-

Reception Site _____   _____

Clergyman/Official _100.-_____   _____100.-_____

Other _Sexton -$50 Candle $5._   _____55.-_____

_____   _____

     Total _____ $ 230.00

RENTAL EQUIPMENT

Tables _____ _____

Chairs _____ _____

Tents _____ _____

Linens _____ _____

China _____ _____

Flatware _____ _____

Other _____ _____

Total _____ _____

GIFTS

Groom _+ Ring Bearer_____ _____95.00_____

Attendants _____ _____96.00_____

Other _Organist + Soloist_ 25 40._____65.00_____

Total _____ $256.00

MISCELLANEOUS

Transportation _____ _____

Housing _____ _____

Other _____ _____

_____ _____

_____ _____

_____ _____

Total _____ _____

Grand Total _____ _____

CHAPTER 3

For Easy Reference

You may want to place these pages at the front of the binder to make the important names and numbers even more easily accessible.

Date of Wedding _May 11, 1991_

Site of Wedding _Calvin Memorial Chapter_

Contact _Rev. Parry_ Phone _843-8041_

Site of Reception _Country Club of York_

Contact _Mr. Cummings_ Phone _____

Officiator _____ Phone _____

Stationer _____

Contact _____ Phone _____

Calligrapher _____ Phone _____

Florist _Ladybug Florist_

Contact _Sheri_ Phone _792-0840_

Caterer _Country Club_

Contact _____ Phone _____

Photographer _Frank E. King_

Contact _____ Phone _292-3515_

Videographer _____

Contact _____ Phone _____

Liquor Service _____

Contact _____ Phone _____

Bakery _Linda's Cake Shop_____

Contact _Linda Williams_____ Phone _792-3433_

Rental Equipment _____

Contact _____Janis McCauley-Organist____ Phone _____

Ceremony Musicians _Andrea Keith-Soloist_____

Contact _____ Phone _____

Reception Musicians _Dave Winter_____

Contact _____ Phone _292-5033_

Bridal Gown _Pat Morgart_____ **Store** _767-4864_

Contact _____ Phone _____

Fittings _____ Delivery _____

Bridesmaids' Gowns _Buttons & Bows_ Store _____

Contact _____ Phone _____

Fittings _____ Delivery _____

Formalwear Rental Shop _Formal Affairs_____

Contact _____ Phone _848-5014_

Fittings _____ Delivery _____

Hotel _____ Room Rate _____

Contact _____ Phone _____

Limousine/Bus Company _____

Contact _____ Phone _____

Gift Registry/Store _____

Contact _____ Phone _____

CHAPTER 4

Organizing the Ceremony and Reception

*B*efore you make your first phone call, there are some very basic decisions that must be made. Sit down with your fiancé and your families and decide upon the date of the wedding, the size and degree of formality of the ceremony and reception, and your budget. Flexibility is important here! Your fiancé's family had hoped to include more of their friends? Perhaps they'd be willing to shoulder more of the expense. You envision an intimate service, but your parents have always imagined a "big event"? Compromise with a family-only ceremony and a grand reception.

It's a good idea to have a few alternate dates in mind. If you've always dreamed of being married by your family minister, you may have to change your schedule to suit his. Or you may find that the one weekend those beautiful gardens are available is the one weekend your former college roommate can't make it. Our big decision came when we found out that the large ballroom at the beautifully restored Peabody Hotel in Memphis was unavailable on the day of our wedding. It was early enough to switch the date, but we decided to use a different room instead.

Once you have the date, sites, and a general idea of your budget, you can begin selecting the professionals who will make your wedding so special: the caterer, florist, photographer, and musicians. Our worksheets will help you keep track of their estimates, and will remind you of the important questions you should ask., A word of advice: If you have a good idea of what you want, say so, but do be open-minded. These people have handled many weddings, and may have ideas that will suit your style beautifully.

Clergyman/Officiator

Most clergymen will want to meet with the bride and groom as early as possible, so this should be the first call you make. This is particularly important if there are any religious differences between the two families, but it is a good idea to discuss the ceremony and music with whomever you have chosen to perform the service.

Name _Rev. Burton J. Parry_

Wife's Name _____

Address _404 W. Market St._

Phone _846-4641_

Dates Available for Ceremony _____

Date Selected _May 11, 1991_

Appointments with Bride and Groom _Feb. 20   4:15_

_____

_____

_____

_____

_____

_____

_____

_____

A donation is often made to the church or synagogue after the ceremony in lieu of a fee. The amount may vary, depending upon the size and degree of formality of your ceremony.

Donation/Fee _$230. 00_

The Ceremony Site

Generally this will be a church or synagogue, but it might well be a hotel, club, or private home. As soon as the engagement is official, you should begin making calls to make certain that the location is available on the date you want.

Ceremony Site _First Presbyterian Church of York_ _Calvin Memorial Chapel_

Address _225 E. Market St. York_

Phone _843-8041_

Church Secretary/ Hotel Manager _____

Fees _$230.00_

Dates Available _____

Date Selected _May 11, 1991_

Date and Time of Rehearsal _May, 10   7 pm._

People Needed for Rehearsal _Kathy_   _Dale_
_____Mom, Rick_   _Dequay, Edith_
_____Michele Miller_   _John Miller_
_____Diane Medlock_   _George Wolf - Acroley_
_____Missy Bottomley_   _Scott Snyder_
X Andrea Keith   _Travis Laughman_

The Wedding Vows and Readings

While writing your own vows is somewhat out of favor, many people feel that it gives freshness and meaning to the wedding ceremony. You may also want to consider asking friends or family members to give readings at the service. A favorite poem, Bible verse, or essay read by a close friend can be a very moving part of the service.

THE VOWS

_____

_____

_____

_____

_____

_____

_____

_____

_____

_____

_____

THE READINGS

Reader _____ Selection _____

Reader _____ Selection _____

Reader _____ Selection _____

Reader _____ Selection _____

Reader _____ Selection _____

Reader _____ Selection _____

The Reception Site

Your reception may be held in the same place as the wedding. This is usually the case when the ceremony is performed at a club or hotel, but it's also possible that your church or synagogue has a room that would be suitable and perhaps more economical.

Site _Country Club of York_

Address _Country Club Rd, Ext._

York, Pa.

Phone _843-8078_

Manager _Mr. Cummings_

Fee/Hour _____ Total Fee _____

Services Provided for Fee _____

_____

_____

_____

Services Provided for Extra Cost _____

_____

_____

_____

Parking Manager_____

☐ Gratuities Included   ☐ Extra

Personnel to Be Tipped _____

_____

_____

22

Selecting the Florist

A wedding without flowers is unimaginable; they add beauty to any ceremony. Your florist should be able to make the most of your budget, whatever its limit. If finances are tight, just keep the choices simple and, almost more importantly, in season.

Florists tend to get booked early, particularly for the peak wedding months, so select one as soon as possible. As you interview florists, ask to see their book. Photographs of past weddings will give you a sense of their style and creativity and may give you an idea of what can be done for your budget. You will probably want to get estimates on the most basic items, and we have provided worksheets for that purpose. A separate sheet with a more detailed breakdown of the types of arrangements you might want to consider (don't forget corsages and boutonnieres for special friends and relatives) is also included; use it to keep track of your final decisions.

When you meet with your florist, you will want to discuss the style of your wedding (is it to be a garden setting or, perhaps, Victorian in mood?) and your color scheme. Bring fabric samples as soon as you have them. Describe the bridal and bridesmaids' gowns (and the bride if she can't be present) to be sure bouquets will be complementary. Find out what other services the florist can provide. Many offer aisle canvases, pew markers, candles, decorations for the cake, cutting knife and table, and other items. Remember to set up an appointment with your florist to visit the ceremony and reception sites if he is not familiar with them.

A final note: Be sure to check with members of the wedding party about allergies. At one wedding we attended, the bridesmaids carried charming nosegays of wildflowers. Charming except for the red-eyed sneezing woman who was allergic to them!

FLORIST ESTIMATE

Shop _Ladybug Florist_

Address _5190 W. Market St. Thomasville_

Phone _792-0840_

Contact _Sheri_

Appointment Scheduled _1/29 3:00_

ALTAR FLOWERS

Type _Baskets w/ white daisies yellow buttons_ Price _____

BRIDAL BOUQUET

Type _White daisies, yellow buttons, green "broom sticks"_ Price _____

BRIDESMAIDS' BOUQUETS

Type _same as brides but smaller_ Price _____

TABLE ARRANGEMENTS FOR RECEPTION

Type _candle w/ glass hurricane cover greens & daisies_ Price _____

OTHER ACCESSORIES

Cake: _fresh daisies + greens_ Price _____

around entire cake Price _____

on table, sm. throw Price _____

bouquet of fresh Price _____

daisies on top of cake Price _____

Notes _____

_____

_____

_____

24

FLORIST ESTIMATE

Shop _____

Address _____

Phone _____

Contact _____

Appointment Scheduled _____

ALTAR FLOWERS

Type _____ Price _____

BRIDAL BOUQUET

Type _____ Price _____

BRIDESMAIDS' BOUQUETS

Type _____ Price _____

TABLE ARRANGEMENTS FOR RECEPTION

Type _____ Price _____

OTHER ACCESSORIES

_____ Price _____

_____ Price _____

_____ Price _____

_____ Price _____

_____ Price _____

Notes _____

_____

_____

_____

The Florist

This page provides a more detailed breakdown of the types of arrangements and flowers you might want to include. Discuss these with the florist you have selected.

Special for Dad - Red Rose with greens + Baby Brea in Bud

DESCRIPTION	PRICE

Altar/Aisle Flowers *2 Baskets, Altar table Candlebria's,*

Bridal Bouquet _____

Bridesmaids' Bouquets/# *3* _____

Bridesmaids' Hair Ornaments/# _____

Corsages for *Mother's + Grandma's.* _____

Boutonnieres for *7b* _____

Flowers for Cake, Table, Knife _____

Centerpiece for Bridal Table _____

Centerpiece for Buffet Table _____

Centerpieces for Guest Tables/# _____

Other Flowers *Corsage for Andrea* _____

Accessories and Other Services

Candles _____

Carpets _____

Ribbons *Made by Jean Hrosa for pews and for Bridal table at reception.*

_____

_____

_____

26

Once you have made your final selection, you should schedule several appointments with your florist. Use this page to keep track of these dates. Remember to take any fabric samples or pictures that you might want to discuss with him.

Appointment with Bride and/or Mother _____

Appointment to Visit Ceremony Site _____

Appointment to Visit Reception Site _____

Delivery Schedule/Set-up Time_____

_____

_____

_____

Selecting a Caterer

Regardless of where your reception is held, you want the food and service to be memorable and special, so selecting the right caterer is of the utmost importance.

You may have already decided that you would like the reception to be at a private home, in a room at the church, or at some other spot that doesn't offer its own food service. In that case you will be dealing with caterers who will plan, prepare, and deliver the food to the reception site. You might prefer, however, to have the reception at a hotel, private club, or other such place that will expect you to make use of their kitchen and staff. In either case the basic selection approach remains the same. Shop around, ask questions, and test-taste!

You will want to discuss the size and type of meal you wish to offer. Is it to be a sit-down dinner, or would a buffet be more economical? A wedding breakfast or an afternoon tea? A good caterer can give you advice as to what menu would be most appropriate and make the best use of your budget.

Find out what services are included. How many waiters and bartenders are provided and at what cost? Will you need to rent or borrow serving pieces, tables, chairs, or other equipment? What color table linens are provided? Are glassware, china, and silver part of the package? Is there a bottle charge if you provide your own wine or champagne? Can a wedding cake be supplied, or must you order that elsewhere? Are taxes and gratuities extra? Get everything in writing and you will minimize the surprises that somehow always seem to accompany the final bill.

CATERER ESTIMATE

Name _Country Club of York_

Address _____

Phone _____

Contact _____

Price per Person _15.25_ Total Price _____

Menu _____

Beverages and Price, if Extra _____

Punch _____ Soft Drinks _____

Coffee/Tea _____ Bottle Charge _____

Services _____

	INCLUDED	EXTRA	UNAVAILABLE
Plates	☑	_____	☐
Flatware	☑	_____	☐
Table Linens	☑	_____	☐
Crystal	☑	_____	☐
Serving Pieces	☑	_____	☐
Bartenders/Waiters	☐	_____	☐
Tables	☑	_____	☐
Chairs	☑	_____	☐
Gratuities	☐	_____	☐

Appointment Scheduled _____

Guest Count Deadline _____

28

CATERER ESTIMATE

Name _____

Address _____

Phone _____

Contact _____

Price per Person _____Total Price _____

Menu _____

Beverages and Price, if Extra _____

Punch _____Soft Drinks _____

Coffee/Tea _____Bottle Charge _____

Services _____

	INCLUDED	EXTRA	UNAVAILABLE
Plates	☐	_____	☐
Flatware	☐	_____	☐
Table Linens	☐	_____	☐
Crystal	☐	_____	☐
Serving Pieces	☐	_____	☐
Bartenders/Waiters	☐	_____	☐
Tables	☐	_____	☐
Chairs	☐	_____	☐
Gratuities	☐	_____	☐

Appointment Scheduled _____

Guest Count Deadline _____

CATERER ESTIMATE

Name _____

Address _____

Phone _____

Contact _____

Price per Person _____Total Price _____

Menu _____

Beverages and Price, if Extra _____

Punch _____Soft Drinks _____

Coffee/Tea _____Bottle Charge _____

Services _____

	INCLUDED	EXTRA	UNAVAILABLE
Plates	☐	_____	☐
Flatware	☐	_____	☐
Table Linens	☐	_____	☐
Crystal	☐	_____	☐
Serving Pieces	☐	_____	☐
Bartenders/Waiters	☐	_____	☐
Tables	☐	_____	☐
Chairs	☐	_____	☐
Gratuities	☐	_____	☐

Appointment Scheduled _____

Guest Count Deadline _____

The Wedding Cake and Groom's Cake

Some caterers will provide one or both of these, but you might still prefer a bakery. The groom's cake, to be taken home by guests in boxes, is optional, but worth considering. Be sure to test-taste!

Bakery _Linda's Cake Shop_

Address _____

Phone _____

Contact _____

WEDDING CAKE

Type of Decoration _All white icing + fresh flowers_

Size and Number of Layers _5 layers_

Number Served _180_ Flavor _Pineapple + Orange_

Delivery Service ☑ Yes ☐ No

To Be Picked Up _____

Ordering Deadline _____ Price _185.–_

GROOM'S CAKE

Description _____ Flavor _____

Number Served _____ Price _____

31

Liquor

You may want to hold several tastings with your fiancé or family to select the champagne or wine for those important toasts!

Champagne/Wine _André_

Cost per Case _____

Where Purchased _____

Description _____

Champagne/Wine _Chablis_

Cost per Case _____

Where Purchased _____

Description _____

Champagne/Wine _____

Cost per Case _____

Where Purchased _____

Description _____

Champagne/Wine _____

Cost per Case _____

Where Purchased _____

Description _____

Champagne/Wine _____

Cost per Case _____

Where Purchased _____

Description _____

Your liquor store can guide you in estimating your needs. Remember that it is better to overestimate—unopened liquor can be returned.

Store _____Phone _____

TYPE OF LIQUOR OR MIXER	# BOTTLES NEEDED	PRICE

Delivery   ☐ Yes   ☐ No   Total   _____

Rental Equipment

Depending upon the site of your reception, you may need to rent equipment and supplies. A hotel will probably provide you with everything you need (for a price, of course), but an outdoor garden setting will leave you starting from scratch. Your caterer may be able to supply you with many of the things you need, but you might find it necessary to deal with a rental company.

RENTAL ESTIMATE

Company _____

Address _____

Phone _____

Contact _____

Tables _____

Chairs _____

Flatware _____

Plates _____

Serving Pieces _____

Linens _____

Tents _____

Dance Floor _____

Other _____

_____

_____

_____

_____

_____

RENTAL ESTIMATE

Company _____

Address _____

Phone _____

Contact _____

Tables _____

Chairs _____

Flatware _____

Plates _____

Serving Pieces _____

Linens _____

Tents _____

Dance Floor _____

Other _____

_____

_____

_____

_____

Selecting a Photographer

If the beauty of your wedding is reflected in its photographs, your wedding album will bring back special memories for years to come.

Be sure to select a photographer with considerable wedding experience. Familiarity with the ceremony and routine should make him more likely to catch every important moment, and less likely to be intrusive. Take a look at samples of his work, and make certain that the photographer whose book you see is the one who will handle your wedding.

Get a complete package price. Find out how many proofs you will be given to select from, how many prints and what sizes are included, as well as the cost of extras. If you wish to have a formal bridal portrait taken in the studio, make those arrangements. (Remember, you'll need your wedding gown for this, so make sure it will be available.)

Discuss the types of pictures you would like to have: Fewer "stock" shots (e.g., looking at the rings) and more reception candids? Lots of soft focus or a straightforward approach? Use the pages provided to make a list of "don't miss" shots for your photographer.

Even if you have engaged a professional, encourage friends with cameras to bring them along. The photographer at our wedding was fine on standard shots, but missed a number of delightful spontaneous moments. Fortunately, a number of guests had cameras, so they captured it all.

Studio _____

Address_____

Phone _____

Contact_____

Price of Wedding Package_____

Number and Sizes of Photos Included _____

Price of Additional Copies _____

Price of Bridal Portrait _____

Notes_____

Studio _____

Address_____

Phone _____

Contact _____

Price of Wedding Package_____

Number and Sizes of Photos Included _____

Price of Additional Copies _____

Price of Bridal Portrait _____

Notes _____

_____

Studio _____

Address_____

Phone _____

Contact _____

Price of Wedding Package_____

Number and Sizes of Photos Included _____

Price of Additional Copies _____

Price of Bridal Portrait _____

Notes _____

PHOTOGRAPHER'S SCHEDULE

Engagement Portrait _____

Formal Bridal Portrait _____

Arrival Time for Wedding_____

PHOTOGRAPHER'S LIST

☐ Bride

☐ Bride and Father

☐ Bride and Mother

☐ Bride and Parents

☐ Bride and Maid of Honor

☐ Bride and Bridesmaids

☐ Bride and Flower Girl

☐ Ring Bearer and Flower Girl

☐ Groom and Groomsmen

☐ Groom and Grandparents

☐ Bride and Groom with Maid of Honor

☐ Bride and Groom with Grandparents

☐ Bride and Groom with Bridesmaids

☐ Sipping the Champagne

☐ Throwing the Garter

☐ Bride and Grandparents

☐ Bride and Sisters

☐ Bride Dressing

☐ Bride with Groom's Parents

☐ Groom

☐ Groom and Father

☐ Groom and Mother

☐ Groom and Best Man

☐ Bride and Groom with Entire Wedding Party

☐ Bride and Groom with Bride's Parents

☐ Bride and Groom with Groom's Parents

☐ Bride and Groom with Best Man

☐ Bride and Groom with Honor Attendants

☐ Cutting the Cake

☐ Throwing the Bouquet

☐ Bride and Groom with Groomsmen

☐ Bride with Groomsmen

☐ Groom with Bridesmaids

☐ Other Groups and Individuals to Be Photographed

_____   _____

_____   _____

_____   _____

_____   _____

_____   _____

_____   _____

_____   _____

_____   _____

_____   _____

Selecting a Videographer

Almost unheard of a decade ago, it is now estimated that nearly a third of the weddings held in the United States each year are videotaped. The majority of these tapes are made by amateurs—guests who were simply asked to bring along the camcorder. But more and more weddings are being recorded by professionals. Look for a videographer who can provide a high-quality product with a minimum of "lights, camera, action" intrusion and be certain that you have approval over the segments that make the final cut, as well as any dubbed-in soundtrack.

Videographer _____

Address_____

Phone _____

Services Offered _____

Fee _____

Fee for Additional Copies _____

Events to Tape _____

_____

Videographer _____

Address_____

Phone _____

Services Offered _____

Fee _____

Fee for Additional Copies _____

Events to Tape _____

_____

_____

Selecting the Musicians

Whether it be a full orchestra or a lone organist, you will no doubt want to have some sort of music at your wedding. There is, of course, a range to suit every budget. You may ask talented friends to perform or depend on the church organist and choir; you might tape some of your own favorites or hire a disc jockey or live musicians.

If you decide to use live musicians, remember that local music schools and universities are good sources of talent, or get references from friends. Interview several groups who perform in the style you prefer; is it classical for the ceremony and swing for the reception? Arrange for an audition, or see if you can drop in on a performance. Once you have decided on a group, make certain that the musicians you heard are the ones who will be playing at your wedding. Many times a bandleader will have a number of different musicians working for him, enabling him to book two different events for the same day and time. Read your contract carefully.

Be sure to specify the type of clothes you would like the band to wear. It could be disconcerting to have your musicians in blue jeans and your guests in black tie. Be certain, too, that you specify whether or not you will feed the band members, and be firm about "groupies." You don't want spouses and girlfriends enjoying your hospitality unexpectedly.

If there are special numbers you would like the musicians to play for either the ceremony or reception, give them plenty of advance notice. They may need time to perfect them.

MUSICIANS ESTIMATE

Name _____

Address _____

Phone _____

Contact _____

Type of Music/Musician _____

☐ Wedding   ☐ Reception

Price per Hour_____Hours Needed _____

Total Cost_____

Special Equipment Needs_____

Audition/Rehearsal Dates _____

MUSICIANS ESTIMATE

Name _____

Address _____

Phone _____

Contact _____

Type of Music/Musician _____

☐ Wedding   ☐ Reception

Price per Hour_____Hours Needed _____

Total Cost_____

Special Equipment Needs_____

Audition/Rehearsal Dates _____

41

MUSICAL SELECTIONS

Photocopy this and give to your musicians.

Wedding _____

Processional _____

Recessional _____

_____

Before the Ceremony _____

_____

_____

_____

_____

During the Ceremony _____

_____

_____

Reception _____

Bride and Groom's Dance _Just You & I — Crystal Gayle + Eddie Ra_

Other _Friends & Lover's — Gloria Loring_

Hold on Loosey — 38 special + anything else by the

Luther Vandross

Old Time Rock + Roll — Bob Segar

It's Rain in Men

Huey Lewis, Reba McEntire

Robert Palmer, Whitney Houston

42

Reception Seating Arrangements

By now your reception plans are well in hand, but there are still a few decisions to be made.

Will you have a receiving line? Many brides dispense with this, preferring to mingle more freely with their guests, but at a large wedding a receiving line can insure that you see everyone, however briefly.

Do you need a seating arrangement? It is essential for a meal with waiter service, as your guests must find their places quickly to expedite service. But you may wish to draw up a seating plan even if the meal is to be served buffet-style. This may be the chance you've been waiting for to see that your college roommate meets your favorite cousin.

You needn't decide who sits next to whom at each table, but you must decide which eight guests (or ten, or whatever number your tables seat) will sit at which table. To simplify seating, make certain that each table is numbered prominently. Then, at a small table at the entrance to the reception, arrange place cards for your guests with their name and table number. The guests can then pick up the card, and find their seats quickly.

Even if you let the guests sit where they like, you will still want to have a special table for the bridal party, and probably one for the parents and/or grandparents of the bride and groom as well.

The Receiving Line _____

_____

_____

_____

_____

_____

_____

_____

_____

_____

_____

RECEPTION—SEATING ARRANGEMENT

Bridal Table

Dale + Kathy Lauchman

Michele Miller

John Miller

Diane Medlock

George Wolf

Missy Bottomley

Scott Snyder

Parents' Table 1

Mom

Rick

Deguay

Edith

Grandma Miller

Grandma Lauchman

Aunt Kay

Uncle Hank

Number of Guest Tables_____14_____

Number per Table_____8 – (three tables of 7)_____

Table # ___2___

Mary Kay

Ted

Karen

Paul

Rob

Tracey – didn't come

Tammy – didn't come

George Coupland – didn't come

Table # ___3___

Jeanne + Richard Andes

Jean + Carl Boyer

Frank + Hazel Addlesberger

Pete + Dee Chantiles

Table # 4

Rocky + Deb Leib
Dave + Joyce Frazier
John Martin + Patti
Pam + Alex

Table # 5

Penny + Tim Treat
Marshall + Ducas Shimmel
Nancy Wolf
Jenny Snyder
Warren

Table # 6

Glen + Rhonda Lauchman
Karen + Jerry Weinholt
Connie + Joe Nonemaker
Kim + Jerry Goodwin

Table # 7

Arlemae Ruppert + (Scott-didn't come)
Bev + Lou Miller - Didn't come
Pat + Carl Lauchman
John Deimler + Wife

47

Table # 8

Kathye, Jeff + Kellye Shue
Wanda, Claude, Travis + Brian
Rick Messinger

Table # 9

Aunt Jean + Bob
Chris Kessler
Dot Kline - didn't come
John + Sue Shupp
Jamie + Missy Shupp

Table # 10

Junior + Connie Cook
Barry + Luann Cook
Kelly + John
Mark + Robin Shupp

Table # 11

Jeanne + Ron Gross
Sue + John Varner
Linda Gross
Tim + Lisa Gross

49

Table # 12

Ronnie + Hilda Herman
Barry + Chris Herman
Karen Hess
Betty Thomas — didn't come
Steve + Lisa Herman — didn't come

Table # 13

Bruce Sowers + Judy
Kevin Bentzel
Mike + Shelby Klindenist
Kathy Aspers (Andrea's Mother)
Andrea Keith

Table # 14

Ken + Pat Baker
Craig + Denny Baker
Denise Weirich + guest
Donaline + Larry Weirich

Table # _____

Table # _____

_____

_____

_____

_____

_____

_____

_____

_____

Table # _____

_____

_____

_____

_____

_____

_____

_____

_____

_____

Table # _____

_____

_____

_____

_____

_____

_____

_____

_____

_____

Table # _____

_____

_____

_____

_____

_____

_____

_____

_____

_____

Table # _____

_____

_____

_____

_____

_____

_____

_____

_____

_____

_____

Table # _____

_____

_____

_____

_____

_____

_____

_____

_____

_____

_____

Table # _____

_____

_____

_____

_____

_____

_____

_____

_____

_____

Table # _____

_____

_____

_____

_____

_____

_____

_____

_____

_____

CHAPTER 5

The Stationer

*U*nless you are named press secretary to the President, you will never order as much stationery for any one event again in your life. Make sure you work with a reputable shop and consider your needs thoroughly.

Does your wedding call for very traditional invitations or something more contemporary or informal? Whatever you decide, be sure to order extras and have the envelopes delivered early to give you a head start on addressing. Remember, too, that some invitation sizes require extra postage; investigate before you order. At one post office we were told our invitations weighed too much and would require extra postage, while at another branch we were assured the extra postage was unnecessary.

You may choose not to send reply cards, but think about sending a self-addressed, stamped postcard to out-of-town guests. Have it printed with fill-ins indicating whether they will be needing a hotel room. This can greatly simplify your planning, as the postcards tend to be returned quickly. You might also want to reproduce maps so that the out-of-towners can get about more easily.

You will probably want personal stationery as well. Stock up on informal note cards for writing those thank-you notes. Consider at-home cards if you will be moving after the wedding.

Order reception favors. You may have always found those monogrammed matchbooks and cocktail napkins a little "cutesy," but when it comes right down to it, you may not feel really married without them!

A final note: Make certain that the stationer sends you a proof of the invitation and/or announcement before it is printed. Check carefully for typos and spelling errors.

Invitations Estimate

Stationer _____

Address _____

Phone _____

Contact _____

Number Needed _____

☐ Embossed   ☐ Engraved

Stock/Color _____

Typeface/Color _____

Size _____ Postage _____

Estimated Cost _____

Reply Cards

☐ Yes   ☐ No

Estimated Cost _____

Envelopes/Return Address

☐ Embossed   ☐ Engraved   ☐ Handwritten

Estimated Cost _____

Total Cost _____

Ordered on _____ Delivery by _____

_____

_____

Invitations Estimate

Stationer _____

Address_____

Phone _____

Contact_____

Number Needed_____

☐ Embossed   ☐ Engraved

Stock/Color_____

Typeface/Color_____

Size _____Postage_____

Estimated Cost_____

Reply Cards

☐ Yes   ☐ No

Estimated Cost_____

Envelopes/Return Address

☐ Embossed   ☐ Engraved   ☐ Handwritten

Estimated Cost_____

Total Cost_____

Ordered on_____Delivery by_____

_____

_____

Announcements

Stationer_____

Address_____

Phone _____

Contact_____

Number needed_____

☐ Embossed   ☐ Engraved

Stock/Color_____

Typeface/Color_____

Size_____Postage_____

Estimated Cost_____

Envelopes/Return Address

☐ Embossed   ☐ Engraved   ☐ Handwritten

Estimated Cost_____

Total Cost_____

Ordered on _____Delivered by_____

Maps/Printed Postcards/Other

Out-of-town guests will appreciate maps, and printed postcards can help you with your planning.

Quantity _____Price_____

Quantity _____Price_____

Quantity _____Price_____

Wedding and Reception Favors

Your stationer can generally supply you with reception favors such as printed cocktail napkins and matchbooks. Be sure to place your order for these items as soon as possible, since they are easily overlooked later.

Cocktail Napkins with Names and Date

Quantity _____ Price _____

Matchbooks/Boxes with Names and Date

Quantity _____ Price _____

Boxes for Groom's Cake with Names and Date

Quantity _____ Price _____

Confetti/Rose Petals/Rice or Rice Bags

Quantity _____ Price _____

Calligrapher Reference

Your stationer may be able to suggest someone to hand-address your invitations and announcements. A beautiful script adds a note of elegance and relieves you of a tedious and time-consuming chore.

Name _____

Phone _____

Estimate/Guest Address _____

Estimate/Return Address _____

Name _____

Phone _____

Estimate/Guest Address _____

Estimate/Return Address _____

Personal Stationery

If you are planning to take your husband's name, you will need to order two sets of informal stationery—one for before the wedding and one for after.

Stationer _____

Address _____

Phone _____

Contact _____

Informal Note Cards

	Maiden Name	Married Name

Number Ordered _____

Imprint or Dye Number _____

Ink Color _____

Stock Color _____

Estimated Price_____Delivery by _____

At-Home Cards

Number Ordered _____

Stock _____Color _____

Embossed _____Engraved _____

Ink Color _____Size _____

Estimated Price_____Delivery by _____

_____

_____

_____

CHAPTER 6

Dressing the Wedding Party

*T*here are several factors to consider when selecting your gown and the attire for the rest of the wedding party. The most obvious, the degree of formality and time of day, will generally dictate whether your groom and his party will be in tuxedos, cutaways, or dark suits; whether you and your maids will be in long gowns or short; and perhaps how long your train will be. But as in all other stages of planning, flexibility plays a role here too. If your fiancé feels ridiculous in a morning suit, then he could consider switching to a tuxedo. Even if he wants to wear a blazer and white pants, this won't necessarily preclude your more formal gown. Strive for balance and compromise.

Take your time as you look for your wedding gown, but remember, if your dress must be special-ordered, it can take three months. This will be the most important dress you will ever buy, and it should be the dress of your dreams! It should not only be beautiful, it should make you feel beautiful. And it needn't be pure white. Stunning gowns come in many shades, from cream and ivory to soft pastels. When you go shopping, remember to wear makeup and have your hair in a style similar to what you plan for the wedding. Take along good shoes and lingerie. These things can make an enormous difference in the way you look to yourself as you try on the dresses.

Shopping for bridesmaids' dresses can present a problem. Bridesmaids generally come in different sizes and shapes, and it's not always easy to find a style to please everyone. And since they usually pay for their own dresses, you have to consider the price as well. You may want your maid of honor to stand out from your bridesmaids. Her dress might be in a different, but complementary style, or perhaps the same dress in a slightly different shade or set off with a contrasting sash. If her dress is identical in every respect, consider having her carry an extra-special bouquet.

Finally, as you shop, keep in mind the setting and the season. The pale pink dress you love for your bridesmaids might be overpowered in a dark cathedral, and while you may have always dreamed of wearing slipper satin, you'll find it awfully uncomfortable if your wedding is in August.

BRIDAL GOWN ESTIMATE

Store _____

Address _____

Phone _____

Contact _____

Designer/Manufacturer _____

Description _____

Price _____ Order by _____

Veil/Hat

Description _____

Price _____ Order by _____

Other Accessories

Description _____

Price _____ Order by _____

Fitting Schedule _____

Notes _____

_____

_____

_____

_____

BRIDAL GOWN ESTIMATE

Store _____

Address _____

Phone _____

Contact _____

Designer/Manufacturer _____

Description _____

Price _____ Order by _____

Veil/Hat

Description _____

Price _____ Order by _____

Other Accessories

Description _____

Price _____ Order by _____

Fitting Schedule _____

Notes _____

_____

_____

_____

_____

_____

_____

BRIDAL GOWN ESTIMATE

Store _____

Address _____

Phone _____

Contact _____

Designer/Manufacturer _____

Description _____

Price _____ Order by _____

Veil/Hat

Description _____

Price _____ Order by _____

Other Accessories

Description _____

Price _____ Order by _____

Fitting Schedule _____

Notes _____

Bride's Checklist

Use this checklist to make sure you have all the essentials!

☐ Gown	☐ Garter
☐ Shoes	☐ Jewelry
☐ Veil/Hat	☐ Something Old
☐ Gloves	☐ Something New
☐ Full Slip	☐ Something Borrowed
☐ Lingerie	☐ Something Blue
☐ Stockings	☐ Flowers

BRIDAL MAGAZINES

Bridal magazines present the latest styles in gowns for you and your attendants. Cut out the pages with the dresses you like and insert them here. Then write down which shops in your hometown carry them.

Magazine _____

Issue/Page _____

Designer _____

Store _____

Phone _____

Magazine _____

Issue/Page _____

Designer _____

Store _____

Phone _____

Magazine _____

Issue/Page _____

Designer _____

Store _____

Phone _____

Magazine _____

Issue/Page _____

Designer _____

Store _____

Phone _____

The Attendants' Responsibilities

The number of attendants you select generally reflects the size and formality of your wedding. The number of ushers and bridesmaids need not match, though the recessional looks better if it does. As a rule of thumb, there should be one usher for every fifty guests. Ushers are responsible for seating the guests, while the bridesmaids have few duties other than looking lovely. It is always a nice touch to include the groom's sisters among the bridesmaids.

The maid/matron of honor and best man have the most responsibility. She holds the bride's bouquet, adjusts her veil, and carries the groom's ring, if it is a double ring ceremony. The best man assists the groom on the wedding day, helps him dress, and likewise carries the bride's ring. He always makes a toast to the bride and groom and often serves as toastmaster at the reception.

Many brides like to include young relatives as flower girls and ring bearers, but, remember, they sometimes steal the show.

BRIDESMAIDS AND MAID OF HONOR—SIZES

Name_____

Address_____

Phone _____

Dress Size_____ Shoe Size_____

Glove Size _____ Hat Size_____

Name_____

Address_____

Phone _____

Dress Size_____ Shoe Size_____

Glove Size _____ Hat Size_____

BRIDESMAIDS AND MAID OF HONOR—SIZES

Name_____

Address_____

Phone _____

Dress Size_____Shoe Size_____

Glove Size _____Hat Size_____

Name_____

Address_____

Phone _____

Dress Size_____Shoe Size_____

Glove Size _____Hat Size_____

Name_____

Address_____

Phone _____

Dress Size_____Shoe Size_____

Glove Size _____Hat Size_____

Name_____

Address_____

Phone _____

Dress Size_____Shoe Size_____

Glove Size _____Hat Size_____

_____

_____

BRIDESMAIDS' AND MAID OF HONOR'S GOWNS ESTIMATE

Store _____

Address _____

Phone _____

Contact _____

Designer/Style Number _____

Description _____

Price _____ Order by _____

Hat Description _____

Price _____ Order by _____

Accessories _____

_____

BRIDESMAIDS' AND MAID OF HONOR'S GOWNS ESTIMATE

Store _____

Address _____

Phone _____

Contact _____

Designer/Style Number _____

Description _____

Price _____ Order by _____

Hat Description _____

Price _____ Order by _____

Accessories _____

BRIDESMAIDS' AND MAID OF HONOR'S GOWNS ESTIMATE

Store _____

Address _____

Phone _____

Contact _____

Designer/Style Number _____

Description _____

Price _____ Order by _____

Hat Description _____

Price _____ Order by _____

Accessories _____

BRIDESMAIDS' AND MAID OF HONOR'S GOWNS ESTIMATE

Store _____

Address _____

Phone _____

Contact _____

Designer/Style Number _____

Description _____

Price _____ Order by _____

Hat Description _____

Price _____ Order by _____

Accessories _____

The Groom's Party

Unless the men in the groom's party will be wearing their own clothes, sizes will be needed for the rental shop. Send a postcard to each and have them fill in the following (gloves and hats are optional; shoe size needed only if they have no black dress shoes):

GROOM'S SIZES

Jacket _____ Sleeve _____

Collar _____ Waist _____

Pants Inseam _____ Shoe _____

Hat _____ Glove _____

FATHER OF THE BRIDE'S SIZES

Jacket _____ Sleeve _____

Collar _____ Waist _____

Pants Inseam _____ Shoe _____

Hat _____ Glove _____

BEST MAN'S SIZES

Name _____

Address _____

Phone _____

Jacket _____ Sleeve _____

Collar _____ Waist _____

Pants Inseam _____ Shoe _____

Hat _____ Glove _____

GROOMSMEN'S/USHERS' SIZES

Name_____

Address_____

Phone _____

Jacket _____Sleeve _____

Collar _____Waist _____

Pants Inseam _____Shoe _____

Hat _____Glove _____

GROOMSMEN'S/USHERS' SIZES

Name_____

Address_____

Phone _____

Jacket _____Sleeve _____

Collar _____Waist _____

Pants Inseam _____Shoe _____

Hat _____Glove _____

GROOMSMEN'S/USHERS' SIZES

Name_____

Address_____

Phone _____

Jacket _____Sleeve _____

Collar _____Waist _____

Pants Inseam _____Shoe _____

Hat _____Glove _____

GROOMSMEN'S/USHERS' SIZES

Name_____

Address_____

Phone _____

Jacket _____Sleeve _____

Collar _____Waist _____

Pants Inseam _____Shoe _____

Hat _____Glove _____

GROOMSMEN'S/USHERS' SIZES

Name_____

Address_____

Phone _____

Jacket _____Sleeve _____

Collar _____Waist _____

Pants Inseam _____Shoe _____

Hat _____Glove _____

GROOMSMEN'S/USHERS' SIZES

Name_____

Address_____

Phone _____

Jacket _____Sleeve _____

Collar _____Waist _____

Pants Inseam _____Shoe _____

Hat _____Glove _____

FORMALWEAR RENTAL INFORMATION

Store_____

Address_____

Phone _____

Contact _____

Description of Formalwear_____

Number Needed _____Rental Fee_____

Provisions for Fittings_____

Order by_____Will Deliver_____

Must Pick up by_____Return by_____

FORMALWEAR RENTAL INFORMATION

Store_____

Address_____

Phone _____

Contact _____

Description of Formalwear_____

Number Needed _____Rental Fee_____

Provisions for Fittings_____

Order by_____Will Deliver_____

Must Pick up by_____Return by_____

CHAPTER 7

Prenuptial Festivities

*T*here will undoubtedly be many people who will want to honor you and your fiancé with parties. This is all part of the fun, so accept graciously and enjoy. A typical schedule might include an engagement party hosted by your parents, a rehearsal dinner given by your fiancé's parents, several showers given by close friends, wedding weekend parties arranged by friends of your parents, and a bridesmaids' lunch planned by you.

Before you make any plans final, however, think carefully. Too many parties just before the wedding could exhaust you. Perhaps you should suggest that several friends co-host one party. An aunt of ours who wanted to "do something" set up a hospitality suite at the hotel where the out-of-town guests were staying, a room where they could gather for coffee and doughnuts in the morning and drinks at night. It worked wonderfully.

Scheduling showers presents a particular problem in that guests are obligated to bring a gift. This can get to be a real financial burden before they've even bought you a wedding present. Be sensible and see to it that different friends are invited to different showers or make it clear that you don't expect a gift at each.

Out-of-town guests may have traveled a long distance for your wedding, so it's nice to fill the weekend with activities. If it is impossible to have all of them at your rehearsal dinner, make certain that there is another event or supper scheduled for them that evening. We had a progressive lunch and bus tour of the city the day before the wedding; it sounded hokey, but turned out to be great fun. It was also a way for several hosts to entertain. These wedding weekend activities give your guests a chance to get to know one another and see some of your hometown. By the time of the actual ceremony, they will all feel like family.

THE ENGAGEMENT PARTY

Parents usually give this party for their daughter. Though it is normally held at home for relatives and close friends, it can be quite elaborate. In that case, you may find it helpful to supplement the following fill-in chart with pages from the section on planning the reception. Simply photocopy the appropriate pages and insert here.

Date/Time _____

Location _____Phone_____

Caterer _____Phone_____

Menu _____

_____

_____

_____

_____

_____

_____

_____

_____

_____

Musicians_____Phone_____

Florist _____Phone_____

GUEST LIST

_____

_____

_____

_____

_____

_____

_____

_____

_____

_____

_____

_____

_____

_____

_____

_____

_____

_____

_____

_____

_____

_____

GUEST LIST

_____

_____

_____

_____

_____

_____

_____

_____

_____

_____

_____

_____

_____

_____

_____

_____

_____

_____

_____

_____

THE REHEARSAL DINNER

Though it is traditional for the groom's family to host this party, other relatives of the bride may offer to do so.

Date/Time _May 10, 1991_ _7:30 pm._

Location _Family Time Rest._ Phone _____

Hosts _Dequay + Edith Lauchman_

GUEST LIST

_____

_____

_____

_____

_____

_____

_____

_____

_____

_____

_____

_____

_____

_____

_____

_____

_____

GUEST LIST

_____

_____

_____

_____

_____

_____

_____

_____

_____

_____

_____

_____

_____

_____

_____

_____

_____

_____

_____

_____

OTHER PARTIES AND SHOWERS

Type of Party _____

Date/Time _____

Location _____

Hosts _____

GUEST LIST

GUEST LIST

OTHER PARTIES AND SHOWERS

Type of Party _Bridal Shower_

Date/Time _____

Location _Mary Kay House_

Hosts _Michele, Diane, Missy_

GUEST LIST

Mom

Edith

Wanda

Kathye

Penny + Erin

Mary Kay

Tracey

Chris

Kelly

Arlamae

Grandma Miller

Connie Nonemaker

Kim Goodwin

Jean Dellinger

Jean Boyer

GUEST LIST

OTHER PARTIES AND SHOWERS

Type of Party _____

Date/Time _____

Location _____

Hosts _____

GUEST LIST

_____

_____

_____

_____

_____

_____

_____

_____

_____

_____

_____

_____

_____

_____

_____

_____

_____

_____

GUEST LIST

OTHER PARTIES AND SHOWERS

Type of Party _____

Date/Time _____

Location _____

Hosts _____

GUEST LIST

_____

_____

_____

_____

_____

_____

_____

_____

_____

_____

_____

_____

_____

_____

_____

_____

_____

_____

_____

_____

GUEST LIST

CHAPTER 8

The Guests

*D*rawing up a guest list can be absolutely agonizing, so here are some tips that might ease the pain.

Divide the list equally between the bride's and groom's families, or perhaps three ways, with one-third going directly to you and your fiancé. If the groom's family is from out of town, and they know few of their friends and relatives will attend, they may be willing to give you some of their spots.

Make phone calls to close friends and relatives (if you feel comfortable about it) to find out whether or not they will be able to attend. If they know that the date you have selected is out of the question or the distance is too great, they will say so, giving you a bit more leeway as you make your final list.

Don't invite one member from a group or set of friends without including the others, unless it is someone to whom you are particularly close and everyone knows it. Otherwise you risk some hurt feelings.

Fiancés and spouses of friends are always included in the guest list. Less formal partners can be invited at your discretion, but if a couple is actually living together, it would be tough to invite one without the other. A casual boyfriend or girlfriend can be included if you'd like to have him or her, but there is no obligation. Just explain your decision to your friend before the invitations go out. She may be delighted with the chance to meet some new people "unencumbered." And don't forget that the clergyman and his wife are both invited to the reception (and, of course, the ceremony!) as are the parents of any children who are attendants at the ceremony.

The following master list should be alphabetized and a copy should be given to whoever is responsible for addressing the invitations. For this reason it is important that spellings here are double-checked and that names and addresses are written out in full. When addressing wedding invitations, the only acceptable abbreviations are Mr., Mrs., Ms., and Dr.

Some couples choose to have a private ceremony followed by a larger reception. You can indicate which guests are to receive an invitation to both events by putting an asterisk or checkmark next to their names.

Guest List

Name Frank & Hazel Addlesberger

Address 865 Taxville Rd. York

Number Attending_____ Needs Accommodations_____

Gift # _____ Gift Description _____

Store Where Purchased_____ Date Acknowledged _____

Name Mr. & Mrs. Gene Almoney

Address R.D. #11 York

Number Attending_____ Needs Accommodations_____

Gift # _____ Gift Description _____

Store Where Purchased_____ Date Acknowledged _____

Name Kelly Altland & guest

Address 1226 W. Market St. York

Number Attending_____ Needs Accommodations_____

Gift # _____ Gift Description _____

Store Where Purchased_____ Date Acknowledged _____

Name Jeanne & Richard Andes

Address 558 Fairview Terrace York

Number Attending_____ Needs Accommodations_____

Gift # _____ Gift Description _____

Store Where Purchased_____ Date Acknowledged _____

GUEST LIST

Name *Ken + Pat Baker + family*

Address *195 W. Hanover Rd. Spring Grove*

Number Attending_____   Needs Accommodations_____

Gift # _____   Gift Description _____

Store Where Purchased_____   Date Acknowledged _____

Name *Rob + Missy Bottomley*

Address_____

Number Attending_____   Needs Accommodations_____

Gift # _____   Gift Description _____

Store Where Purchased_____   Date Acknowledged _____

Name *Dick + Roe Becker*

Address_____

Number Attending_____   Needs Accommodations_____

Gift # _____   Gift Description _____

Store Where Purchased_____   Date Acknowledged _____

Name *Jean + Carl Boyer*

Address *1786 Marigold Rd York 17404*

Number Attending_____   Needs Accommodations_____

Gift # _____   Gift Description _____

Store Where Purchased_____   Date Acknowledged _____

91

GUEST LIST

Name_____

Address_____

Number Attending_____   Needs Accommodations_____

Gift # _____   Gift Description _____

Store Where Purchased_____   Date Acknowledged _____

Name_____

Address_____

Number Attending_____   Needs Accommodations_____

Gift # _____   Gift Description _____

Store Where Purchased_____   Date Acknowledged _____

Name_____

Address_____

Number Attending_____   Needs Accommodations_____

Gift # _____   Gift Description _____

Store Where Purchased_____   Date Acknowledged _____

Name_____

Address_____

Number Attending_____   Needs Accommodations_____

Gift # _____   Gift Description _____

Store Where Purchased_____   Date Acknowledged _____

GUEST LIST

Name_____

Address_____

Number Attending_____   Needs Accommodations_____

Gift # _____   Gift Description _____

Store Where Purchased_____   Date Acknowledged _____

Name_____

Address_____

Number Attending_____   Needs Accommodations_____

Gift # _____   Gift Description _____

Store Where Purchased_____   Date Acknowledged _____

Name_____

Address_____

Number Attending_____   Needs Accommodations_____

Gift # _____   Gift Description _____

Store Where Purchased_____   Date Acknowledged _____

Name_____

Address_____

Number Attending_____   Needs Accommodations_____

Gift # _____   Gift Description _____

Store Where Purchased_____   Date Acknowledged _____

GUEST LIST

Name _Dorcas & Dave Brodbeck_

Address _R.D. #1 Seven Valleys 17360_

Number Attending _____ Needs Accommodations _____

Gift # _____ Gift Description _____

Store Where Purchased _____ Date Acknowledged _____

Name _Ivan Beatty & Kathy_

Address _____

Number Attending _____ Needs Accommodations _____

Gift # _____ Gift Description _____

Store Where Purchased _____ Date Acknowledged _____

Name _Irvin Bentzel + guest_

Address _738 Cleveland Ave, York 17403_

Number Attending _____ Needs Accommodations _____

Gift # _____ Gift Description _____

Store Where Purchased _____ Date Acknowledged _____

Name _Luther Beam_

Address _2172 High St. York_

Number Attending _____ Needs Accommodations _____

Gift # _____ Gift Description _____

Store Where Purchased _____ Date Acknowledged _____

GUEST LIST

Name *Martin & Connie Cook*

Address *1625 South Dr. York*

Number Attending_____ Needs Accommodations_____

Gift # _____ Gift Description _____

Store Where Purchased_____ Date Acknowledged _____

Name *Barry & Luann Cook*

Address *426 Leaman Lane Hallam*

Number Attending_____ Needs Accommodations_____

Gift # _____ Gift Description _____

Store Where Purchased_____ Date Acknowledged _____

Name *Tracey Cook & guest*

Address_____

Number Attending_____ Needs Accommodations_____

Gift # _____ Gift Description _____

Store Where Purchased_____ Date Acknowledged _____

Name *Tammy Cook & guest*

Address_____

Number Attending_____ Needs Accommodations_____

Gift # _____ Gift Description _____

Store Where Purchased_____ Date Acknowledged _____

95

GUEST LIST

Name Marlene Cook + John
_____

Address_____

Number Attending_____   Needs Accommodations_____

Gift # _____   Gift Description _____

Store Where Purchased_____   Date Acknowledged _____

Name George Copeland
_____

Address 2510 Jackson St. Scranton
_____

Number Attending_____   Needs Accommodations_____

Gift # _____   Gift Description _____

Store Where Purchased_____   Date Acknowledged _____

Name Pete + Dee Chantilea
_____

Address 700 Fireside Rd. York
_____

Number Attending_____   Needs Accommodations_____

Gift # _____   Gift Description _____

Store Where Purchased_____   Date Acknowledged _____

Name Jean Dellinger + guest
_____

Address 19 S. Lee St. York
_____

Number Attending_____   Needs Accommodations_____

Gift # _____   Gift Description _____

Store Where Purchased_____   Date Acknowledged _____

GUEST LIST

Name _John Deimler + Wife_

Address _480 North Ridge Rd. Reinholds, Pa 17569_

Number Attending_____ Needs Accommodations_____

Gift #_____ Gift Description _____

Store Where Purchased_____ Date Acknowledged_____

Name _Dave + Joyce Frazier Jr._

Address _R.D. #1 Lehman Rd. Spring Grove, 17362_

Number Attending_____ Needs Accommodations_____

Gift #_____ Gift Description _____

Store Where Purchased_____ Date Acknowledged_____

Name _Warren Furman + guest_

Address_____

Number Attending_____ Needs Accommodations_____

Gift #_____ Gift Description _____

Store Where Purchased_____ Date Acknowledged_____

Name _Mary Kay + Todd Fadely_

Address _137 S. 7th St. Mt. Wolf_

Number Attending_____ Needs Accommodations_____

Gift #_____ Gift Description _____

Store Where Purchased_____ Date Acknowledged_____

GUEST LIST

Name Alice + Stuart Frey

Address 2711 Golf Dr.

Number Attending_____ Needs Accommodations_____

Gift # _____ Gift Description _____

Store Where Purchased_____ Date Acknowledged _____

Name Ron, Jean, Linda Gross

Address R.D. #2   Thomasville

Number Attending_____ Needs Accommodations_____

Gift # _____ Gift Description _____

Store Where Purchased_____ Date Acknowledged _____

Name Linda Gross + guest

Address R.D. #2   Thomasville

Number Attending_____ Needs Accommodations_____

Gift # _____ Gift Description _____

Store Where Purchased_____ Date Acknowledged _____

Name John Gross + guest

Address_____

Number Attending_____ Needs Accommodations_____

Gift # _____ Gift Description _____

Store Where Purchased_____ Date Acknowledged _____

GUEST LIST

Name _Jim + Lisa Gross_

Address_____

Number Attending_____ Needs Accommodations_____

Gift # _____ Gift Description _____

Store Where Purchased_____ Date Acknowledged _____

Name _Kazys + Linda Haciunas_

Address_____

Number Attending_____ Needs Accommodations_____

Gift # _____ Gift Description _____

Store Where Purchased_____ Date Acknowledged _____

Name _Kim + Jerry Goodwin_

Address_____

Number Attending_____ Needs Accommodations_____

Gift # _____ Gift Description _____

Store Where Purchased_____ Date Acknowledged _____

Name _Charles + Mary Hash_

Address_____

Number Attending_____ Needs Accommodations_____

Gift # _____ Gift Description _____

Store Where Purchased_____ Date Acknowledged _____

GUEST LIST

Name _Ann Marie Herman & guest_

Address _____

Number Attending _____ Needs Accommodations _____

Gift # _____ Gift Description _____

Store Where Purchased _____ Date Acknowledged _____

Name _Ronnie & Hilda Herman_

Address _____

Number Attending _____ Needs Accommodations _____

Gift # _____ Gift Description _____

Store Where Purchased _____ Date Acknowledged _____

Name _Steve & Lisa Herman_

Address _____

Number Attending _____ Needs Accommodations _____

Gift # _____ Gift Description _____

Store Where Purchased _____ Date Acknowledged _____

Name _Barry & Chris Herman_

Address _____

Number Attending _____ Needs Accommodations _____

Gift # _____ Gift Description _____

Store Where Purchased _____ Date Acknowledged _____

GUEST LIST

Name Karen Ness & guest

Address

Number Attending_____ Needs Accommodations_____

Gift #_____ Gift Description _____

Store Where Purchased_____ Date Acknowledged_____

Name Mr. & Mrs. Charles Kraft

Address

Number Attending_____ Needs Accommodations_____

Gift #_____ Gift Description _____

Store Where Purchased_____ Date Acknowledged_____

Name Mr. & Mrs. Lawrence Kraft

Address

Number Attending_____ Needs Accommodations_____

Gift #_____ Gift Description _____

Store Where Purchased_____ Date Acknowledged_____

Name Andrea Keith + Mother (Kathy Asper)

Address

Number Attending_____ Needs Accommodations_____

Gift #_____ Gift Description _____

Store Where Purchased_____ Date Acknowledged_____

GUEST LIST

Name Chris & Ilene Kessler

Address_____

Number Attending_____   Needs Accommodations_____

Gift # _____   Gift Description _____

Store Where Purchased_____   Date Acknowledged _____

Name Kay & Hank Krosky

Address_____

Number Attending_____   Needs Accommodations_____

Gift # _____   Gift Description _____

Store Where Purchased_____   Date Acknowledged _____

Name Mike & Shelby Klinedinst

Address_____

Number Attending_____   Needs Accommodations_____

Gift # _____   Gift Description _____

Store Where Purchased_____   Date Acknowledged _____

Name Wanda, Claude, Travis & Brian

Address_____

Number Attending_____   Needs Accommodations_____

Gift # _____   Gift Description _____

Store Where Purchased_____   Date Acknowledged _____

GUEST LIST

Name _Annie Lauchman_

Address _____

Number Attending _____ Needs Accommodations _____

Gift # _____ Gift Description _____

Store Where Purchased _____ Date Acknowledged _____

Name _Carl + Pat Lauchman_

Address _____

Number Attending _____ Needs Accommodations _____

Gift # _____ Gift Description _____

Store Where Purchased _____ Date Acknowledged _____

Name _Glen + Rhonda Lauchman_

Address _____

Number Attending _____ Needs Accommodations _____

Gift # _____ Gift Description _____

Store Where Purchased _____ Date Acknowledged _____

Name _Rocky + Deb Leib_

Address _____

Number Attending _____ Needs Accommodations _____

Gift # _____ Gift Description _____

Store Where Purchased _____ Date Acknowledged _____

103

GUEST LIST

Name _Edith + Deguay Lauchman_

Address _____

Number Attending_____ Needs Accommodations_____

Gift # _____ Gift Description _____

Store Where Purchased_____ Date Acknowledged _____

Name _Paul + Marie Lenty_

Address _____

Number Attending_____ Needs Accommodations_____

Gift # _____ Gift Description _____

Store Where Purchased_____ Date Acknowledged _____

Name _Betty + Bill Moul_

Address _____

Number Attending_____ Needs Accommodations_____

Gift # _____ Gift Description _____

Store Where Purchased_____ Date Acknowledged _____

Name _Diane Medlock + Rick Detwiler_

Address _____

Number Attending_____ Needs Accommodations_____

Gift # _____ Gift Description _____

Store Where Purchased_____ Date Acknowledged _____

GUEST LIST

Name *Karen Mattern + guest*

Address_____

Number Attending_____ Needs Accommodations_____

Gift # _____ Gift Description _____

Store Where Purchased_____ Date Acknowledged _____

Name *Paul + Kathy McAlvin*

Address_____

Number Attending_____ Needs Accommodations_____

Gift # _____ Gift Description _____

Store Where Purchased_____ Date Acknowledged _____

Name *Sarah Miller*

Address_____

Number Attending_____ Needs Accommodations_____

Gift # _____ Gift Description _____

Store Where Purchased_____ Date Acknowledged _____

Name *Lou + Beverly Miller*

Address_____

Number Attending_____ Needs Accommodations_____

Gift # _____ Gift Description _____

Store Where Purchased_____ Date Acknowledged _____

GUEST LIST

Name _Johnnie Martin + guest_

Address_____

Number Attending_____ Needs Accommodations_____

Gift # _____ Gift Description _____

Store Where Purchased_____ Date Acknowledged _____

Name _Rick Messinger) + guest_

Address_____

Number Attending_____ Needs Accommodations_____

Gift # _____ Gift Description _____

Store Where Purchased_____ Date Acknowledged _____

Name _Mary Miller)_

Address_____

Number Attending_____ Needs Accommodations_____

Gift # _____ Gift Description _____

Store Where Purchased_____ Date Acknowledged _____

Name _Mr. + Mrs. Ralph Hess_

Address_____

Number Attending_____ Needs Accommodations_____

Gift # _____ Gift Description _____

Store Where Purchased_____ Date Acknowledged _____

GUEST LIST

Name Mr. & Mrs. Kenneth Nelson

Address_____

Number Attending_____ Needs Accommodations_____

Gift # _____ Gift Description _____

Store Where Purchased_____ Date Acknowledged _____

Name Connie & Joe Noremaker

Address_____

Number Attending_____ Needs Accommodations_____

Gift # _____ Gift Description _____

Store Where Purchased_____ Date Acknowledged _____

Name Rev. Burton Parry & Wife

Address_____

Number Attending_____ Needs Accommodations_____

Gift # _____ Gift Description _____

Store Where Purchased_____ Date Acknowledged _____

Name Arlemae, Earl, Scott & Matthew

Address_____

Number Attending_____ Needs Accommodations_____

Gift # _____ Gift Description _____

Store Where Purchased_____ Date Acknowledged _____

GUEST LIST

Name _Pam Roehm + Alex_

Address _____

Number Attending _____ Needs Accommodations _____

Gift # _____ Gift Description _____

Store Where Purchased _____ Date Acknowledged _____

Name _Laurence + Toot Rizzuto_

Address _____

Number Attending _____ Needs Accommodations _____

Gift # _____ Gift Description _____

Store Where Purchased _____ Date Acknowledged _____

Name _____

Address _____

Number Attending _____ Needs Accommodations _____

Gift # _____ Gift Description _____

Store Where Purchased _____ Date Acknowledged _____

Name _____

Address _____

Number Attending _____ Needs Accommodations _____

Gift # _____ Gift Description _____

Store Where Purchased _____ Date Acknowledged _____

GUEST LIST

Name_____

Address_____

Number Attending_____   Needs Accommodations_____

Gift # _____   Gift Description _____

Store Where Purchased_____   Date Acknowledged _____

Name_____

Address_____

Number Attending_____   Needs Accommodations_____

Gift # _____   Gift Description _____

Store Where Purchased_____   Date Acknowledged _____

Name_____

Address_____

Number Attending_____   Needs Accommodations_____

Gift # _____   Gift Description _____

Store Where Purchased_____   Date Acknowledged _____

Name_____

Address_____

Number Attending_____   Needs Accommodations_____

Gift # _____   Gift Description _____

Store Where Purchased_____   Date Acknowledged _____

109

GUEST LIST

Name_____

Address_____

Number Attending_____   Needs Accommodations_____

Gift # _____   Gift Description _____

Store Where Purchased_____   Date Acknowledged _____

Name_____

Address_____

Number Attending_____   Needs Accommodations_____

Gift # _____   Gift Description _____

Store Where Purchased_____   Date Acknowledged _____

Name_____

Address_____

Number Attending_____   Needs Accommodations_____

Gift # _____   Gift Description _____

Store Where Purchased_____   Date Acknowledged _____

Name_____

Address_____

Number Attending_____   Needs Accommodations_____

Gift # _____   Gift Description _____

Store Where Purchased_____   Date Acknowledged _____

GUEST LIST

Name_____

Address_____

Number Attending_____   Needs Accommodations_____

Gift # _____   Gift Description _____

Store Where Purchased_____   Date Acknowledged _____

Name_____

Address_____

Number Attending_____   Needs Accommodations_____

Gift # _____   Gift Description _____

Store Where Purchased_____   Date Acknowledged _____

Name_____

Address_____

Number Attending_____   Needs Accommodations_____

Gift # _____   Gift Description _____

Store Where Purchased_____   Date Acknowledged _____

Name_____

Address_____

Number Attending_____   Needs Accommodations_____

Gift # _____   Gift Description _____

Store Where Purchased_____   Date Acknowledged _____

GUEST LIST

Name_____

Address_____

Number Attending_____   Needs Accommodations_____

Gift # _____   Gift Description _____

Store Where Purchased_____   Date Acknowledged _____

Name_____

Address_____

Number Attending_____   Needs Accommodations_____

Gift # _____   Gift Description _____

Store Where Purchased_____   Date Acknowledged _____

Name_____

Address_____

Number Attending_____   Needs Accommodations_____

Gift # _____   Gift Description _____

Store Where Purchased_____   Date Acknowledged _____

Name_____

Address_____

Number Attending_____   Needs Accommodations_____

Gift # _____   Gift Description _____

Store Where Purchased_____   Date Acknowledged _____

GUEST LIST

Name_____

Address_____

Number Attending_____   Needs Accommodations_____

Gift # _____   Gift Description _____

Store Where Purchased_____   Date Acknowledged _____

Name_____

Address_____

Number Attending_____   Needs Accommodations_____

Gift # _____   Gift Description _____

Store Where Purchased_____   Date Acknowledged _____

Name_____

Address_____

Number Attending_____   Needs Accommodations_____

Gift # _____   Gift Description _____

Store Where Purchased_____   Date Acknowledged _____

Name_____

Address_____

Number Attending_____   Needs Accommodations_____

Gift # _____   Gift Description _____

Store Where Purchased_____   Date Acknowledged _____

GUEST LIST

Name_____

Address_____

Number Attending_____   Needs Accommodations_____

Gift # _____   Gift Description _____

Store Where Purchased_____   Date Acknowledged _____

Name_____

Address_____

Number Attending_____   Needs Accommodations_____

Gift # _____   Gift Description _____

Store Where Purchased_____   Date Acknowledged _____

Name_____

Address_____

Number Attending_____   Needs Accommodations_____

Gift # _____   Gift Description _____

Store Where Purchased_____   Date Acknowledged _____

Name_____

Address_____

Number Attending_____   Needs Accommodations_____

Gift # _____   Gift Description _____

Store Where Purchased_____   Date Acknowledged _____

GUEST LIST

Name_____

Address_____

Number Attending_____   Needs Accommodations_____

Gift # _____   Gift Description _____

Store Where Purchased_____   Date Acknowledged _____

Name_____

Address_____

Number Attending_____   Needs Accommodations_____

Gift # _____   Gift Description _____

Store Where Purchased_____   Date Acknowledged _____

Name_____

Address_____

Number Attending_____   Needs Accommodations_____

Gift # _____   Gift Description _____

Store Where Purchased_____   Date Acknowledged _____

Name_____

Address_____

Number Attending_____   Needs Accommodations_____

Gift # _____   Gift Description _____

Store Where Purchased_____   Date Acknowledged _____

115

GUEST LIST

Name_____

Address_____

Number Attending_____   Needs Accommodations_____

Gift # _____   Gift Description _____

Store Where Purchased_____   Date Acknowledged _____

Name_____

Address_____

Number Attending_____   Needs Accommodations_____

Gift # _____   Gift Description _____

Store Where Purchased_____   Date Acknowledged _____

Name_____

Address_____

Number Attending_____   Needs Accommodations_____

Gift # _____   Gift Description _____

Store Where Purchased_____   Date Acknowledged _____

Name_____

Address_____

Number Attending_____   Needs Accommodations_____

Gift # _____   Gift Description _____

Store Where Purchased_____   Date Acknowledged _____

GUEST LIST

Name_____

Address_____

Number Attending_____   Needs Accommodations_____

Gift # _____   Gift Description _____

Store Where Purchased_____   Date Acknowledged _____

Name_____

Address_____

Number Attending_____   Needs Accommodations_____

Gift # _____   Gift Description _____

Store Where Purchased_____   Date Acknowledged _____

Name_____

Address_____

Number Attending_____   Needs Accommodations_____

Gift # _____   Gift Description _____

Store Where Purchased_____   Date Acknowledged _____

Name_____

Address_____

Number Attending_____   Needs Accommodations_____

Gift # _____   Gift Description _____

Store Where Purchased_____   Date Acknowledged _____

GUEST LIST

Name_____

Address_____

Number Attending_____   Needs Accommodations_____

Gift # _____   Gift Description _____

Store Where Purchased_____   Date Acknowledged _____

Name_____

Address_____

Number Attending_____   Needs Accommodations_____

Gift # _____   Gift Description _____

Store Where Purchased_____   Date Acknowledged _____

Name_____

Address_____

Number Attending_____   Needs Accommodations_____

Gift # _____   Gift Description _____

Store Where Purchased_____   Date Acknowledged _____

Name_____

Address_____

Number Attending_____   Needs Accommodations_____

Gift # _____   Gift Description _____

Store Where Purchased_____   Date Acknowledged _____

GUEST LIST

Name_____

Address_____

Number Attending_____   Needs Accommodations_____

Gift # _____   Gift Description _____

Store Where Purchased_____   Date Acknowledged _____

Name_____

Address_____

Number Attending_____   Needs Accommodations_____

Gift # _____   Gift Description _____

Store Where Purchased_____   Date Acknowledged _____

Name_____

Address_____

Number Attending_____   Needs Accommodations_____

Gift # _____   Gift Description _____

Store Where Purchased_____   Date Acknowledged _____

Name_____

Address_____

Number Attending_____   Needs Accommodations_____

Gift # _____   Gift Description _____

Store Where Purchased_____   Date Acknowledged _____

GUEST LIST

Name_____

Address_____

Number Attending_____   Needs Accommodations_____

Gift # _____   Gift Description _____

Store Where Purchased_____   Date Acknowledged _____

Name_____

Address_____

Number Attending_____   Needs Accommodations_____

Gift # _____   Gift Description _____

Store Where Purchased_____   Date Acknowledged _____

Name_____

Address_____

Number Attending_____   Needs Accommodations_____

Gift # _____   Gift Description _____

Store Where Purchased_____   Date Acknowledged _____

Name_____

Address_____

Number Attending_____   Needs Accommodations_____

Gift # _____   Gift Description _____

Store Where Purchased_____   Date Acknowledged _____

GUEST LIST

Name_____

Address_____

Number Attending_____   Needs Accommodations_____

Gift # _____   Gift Description _____

Store Where Purchased_____   Date Acknowledged _____

Name_____

Address_____

Number Attending_____   Needs Accommodations_____

Gift # _____   Gift Description _____

Store Where Purchased_____   Date Acknowledged _____

Name_____

Address_____

Number Attending_____   Needs Accommodations_____

Gift # _____   Gift Description _____

Store Where Purchased_____   Date Acknowledged _____

Name_____

Address_____

Number Attending_____   Needs Accommodations_____

Gift # _____   Gift Description _____

Store Where Purchased_____   Date Acknowledged _____

Announcements

If you are planning a very small wedding and reception, you may wish to send out announcements to a wider circle of friends and relatives. Traditionally a wedding announcement does not carry with it a gift obligation, but you may receive gifts from friends who learn of your wedding via an announcement or even word of mouth.

ANNOUNCEMENT LIST

Name_____

Address_____

Name_____

Address_____

Name_____

Address_____

Name_____

Address_____

Name_____

Address_____

Name_____

Address_____

Name_____

Address_____

Name_____

Address_____

Name_____

Address_____

ANNOUNCEMENT LIST

Name_____

Address_____

Name_____

Address_____

Name_____

Address_____

Name_____

Address_____

Name_____

Address_____

Name_____

Address_____

Name_____

Address_____

Name_____

Address_____

Name_____

Address_____

Name_____

Address_____

Name_____

Address_____

ADDITIONAL GIFTS RECEIVED

Gift # _____

Gift Description _____

Received from _____

Store Where Purchased _____

Date Acknowledged _____

Gift # _____

Gift Description _____

Received from _____

Store Where Purchased _____

Date Acknowledged _____

Gift # _____

Gift Description _____

Received from _____

Store Where Purchased _____

Date Acknowledged _____

Gift # _____

Gift Description _____

Received from _____

Store Where Purchased _____

Date Acknowledged _____

ADDITIONAL GIFTS RECEIVED

Gift # _____

Gift Description _____

Received from _____

Store Where Purchased _____

Date Acknowledged _____

Gift # _____

Gift Description _____

Received from _____

Store Where Purchased _____

Date Acknowledged _____

Gift # _____

Gift Description _____

Received from _____

Store Where Purchased _____

Date Acknowledged _____

Gift # _____

Gift Description _____

Received from _____

Store Where Purchased _____

Date Acknowledged _____

ADDITIONAL GIFTS RECEIVED

Gift # _____

Gift Description _____

Received from _____

Store Where Purchased _____

Date Acknowledged _____

Gift # _____

Gift Description _____

Received from _____

Store Where Purchased _____

Date Acknowledged _____

Gift # _____

Gift Description _____

Received from _____

Store Where Purchased _____

Date Acknowledged _____

Gift # _____

Gift Description _____

Received from _____

Store Where Purchased _____

Date Acknowledged _____

GUEST ACCOMMODATIONS

Arrangements should be made for housing out-of-town guests. Some will be staying with friends or relatives, while others will prefer to stay at a hotel.

GUESTS IN HOMES

Guest _____

Staying With_____

Address_____

Phone _____

Will Need Transportation   ☐ Yes   ☐ No

Driver_____

Guest _____

Staying With_____

Address_____

Phone _____

Will Need Transportation   ☐ Yes   ☐ No

Driver_____

Guest _____

Staying With_____

Address_____

Phone _____

Will Need Transportation   ☐ Yes   ☐ No

Driver_____

GUESTS IN HOMES

Guest _____

Staying With_____

Address_____

Phone _____

Will Need Transportation   ☐ Yes   ☐ No

Driver_____

Guest _____

Staying With_____

Address_____

Phone _____

Will Need Transportation   ☐ Yes   ☐ No

Driver_____

Guest _____

Staying With_____

Address_____

Phone _____

Will Need Transportation   ☐ Yes   ☐ No

Driver_____

_____

_____

_____

GUESTS IN HOMES

Guest _____

Staying With_____

Address_____

Phone _____

Will Need Transportation ☐ Yes ☐ No

Driver_____

Guest _____

Staying With_____

Address_____

Phone _____

Will Need Transportation ☐ Yes ☐ No

Driver_____

Guest _____

Staying With_____

Address_____

Phone _____

Will Need Transportation ☐ Yes ☐ No

Driver_____

_____

_____

_____

HOTEL ACCOMMODATIONS

Before making any reservations, check prices. You may be able to get a group rate if you book enough rooms. Be sure to have the hotel send out confirmation cards to all out-of-town guests for whom you have made reservations. Guests are expected to pay for their own rooms.

Consider booking an extra room as a "hospitality suite." Keep it stocked with coffee, soft drinks, and snacks, and guests will feel particularly pampered.

HOTEL ESTIMATES

Hotel_____

Address_____

Phone _____

Contact _____

Room Rate _____

Hotel_____

Address_____

Phone _____

Contact _____

Room Rate _____

Hotel_____

Address_____

Phone _____

Contact _____

Room Rate _____

Final Choice _____

FINAL HOTEL RESERVATION LIST

Guest_____Number Sharing Room_____

Dates Reserved _____Room Number_____

Guest_____Number Sharing Room_____

Dates Reserved _____Room Number_____

Guest_____Number Sharing Room_____

Dates Reserved _____Room Number_____

Guest_____Number Sharing Room_____

Dates Reserved _____Room Number_____

Guest_____Number Sharing Room_____

Dates Reserved _____Room Number_____

Guest_____Number Sharing Room_____

Dates Reserved _____Room Number_____

Guest_____Number Sharing Room_____

Dates Reserved _____Room Number_____

Guest_____Number Sharing Room_____

Dates Reserved _____Room Number_____

Guest_____Number Sharing Room_____

Dates Reserved _____Room Number_____

Guest_____Number Sharing Room_____

Dates Reserved _____Room Number_____

Guest_____Number Sharing Room_____

Dates Reserved _____Room Number_____

Guest_____Number Sharing Room_____

Dates Reserved _____Room Number_____

FINAL HOTEL RESERVATION LIST

Guest_____Number Sharing Room_____

Dates Reserved _____Room Number_____

Guest_____Number Sharing Room_____

Dates Reserved _____Room Number_____

Guest_____Number Sharing Room_____

Dates Reserved _____Room Number_____

Guest_____Number Sharing Room_____

Dates Reserved _____Room Number_____

Guest_____Number Sharing Room_____

Dates Reserved _____Room Number_____

Guest_____Number Sharing Room_____

Dates Reserved _____Room Number_____

Guest_____Number Sharing Room_____

Dates Reserved _____Room Number_____

Guest_____Number Sharing Room_____

Dates Reserved _____Room Number_____

Guest_____Number Sharing Room_____

Dates Reserved _____Room Number_____

Guest_____Number Sharing Room_____

Dates Reserved _____Room Number_____

Transportation

AIRLINE INFORMATION

Guests should make their own travel arrangements to and from the city where the wedding is taking place. It is nice, however, to arrange to have them picked up at the airport, if possible. Siblings of the bride are particularly useful for this.

Guest or Guests _____

Arrival Time _____

Airline/Flight Number _____

To Be Picked up by _____

Staying at _____

Departure Time _____

Airline/Flight Number _____

Guest or Guests _____

Arrival Time _____

Airline/Flight Number _____

To Be Picked up by _____

Staying at _____

Departure Time _____

Airline/Flight Number _____

AIRLINE INFORMATION

Guest or Guests _____

Arrival Time_____

Airline/Flight Number_____

To Be Picked up by_____

Staying at _____

Departure Time _____

Airline/Flight Number_____

Guest or Guests _____

Arrival Time_____

Airline/Flight Number_____

To Be Picked up by_____

Staying at _____

Departure Time _____

Airline/Flight Number_____

Guest or Guests _____

Arrival Time_____

Airline/Flight Number_____

To Be Picked up by_____

Staying at _____

Departure Time _____

Airline/Flight Number_____

BUS AND LIMOUSINE SERVICE

If you have a large number of out-of-town guests, you might consider renting a bus to take them from the hotel to the wedding and other events. You may also want to hire a limousine to transport the bride on her wedding day. Other, more unusual, transportation plans can sometimes be arranged—horse-drawn carriages, antique cars, even hot-air balloons.

Bus Company _____ Phone _____

Contact _____ Rates _____

Limousine _____ Phone _____

Contact _____ Rates _____

Other _____

_____

_____

DRIVER INFORMATION

Friends and relatives can often be pressed into service to pick up guests at the airport and to get them to various events.

Driver _____ Phone _____

Pick up _____ Date/Time _____

at _____ Take to _____

Driver _____ Phone _____

Pick up _____ Date/Time _____

at _____ Take to _____

Driver _____ Phone _____

Pick up _____ Date/Time _____

at _____ Take to _____

DRIVER INFORMATION

Driver _____Phone_____

Pick up _____Date/Time_____

at _____Take to_____

Driver _____Phone_____

Pick up _____Date/Time_____

at _____Take to_____

Driver _____Phone_____

Pick up _____Date/Time_____

at _____Take to_____

Driver _____Phone_____

Pick up _____Date/Time_____

at _____Take to_____

Driver _____Phone_____

Pick up _____Date/Time_____

at _____Take to_____

Driver _____Phone_____

Pick up _____Date/Time_____

at _____Take to_____

Driver _____Phone_____

Pick up _____Date/Time_____

at _____Take to_____

CHAPTER 9

The Gift Registry

*Y*ou will probably want to take advantage of the services of a bridal registry at a department or gift store, or perhaps at several different stores. The gift consultants can help you pick out harmonious table settings as well as other items that will complement your new home and entertaining needs. They will also keep a list of your gift preferences. By calling the gift registry, friends can be certain that they are giving you something you really like and want, and the careful record-keeping will minimize duplication.

When you register your china pattern, see if the store will send cards (e.g., "One Wedgwood Runnymede salad plate from Mr. & Mrs. Phillips") rather than the piece of china itself. You'll still be able to write a prompt note of thanks, and later when you find yourself with ten salad plates, twelve bread and butter plates, and no dinner plates, you won't have to cart fragile china back to the store to even up your place settings. Of course you'll want to have one complete place setting of your china, crystal, and silver at home to show your friends, even if you choose not to display your other gifts.

If a gift arrives damaged, be sure to take it back immediately, along with the packing materials. Many stores will not process claims without the original package. Don't notify the person who gave the gift unless it is clear that he or she packed and insured it personally.

SETTING UP GIFT RECORDS

It is essential that you keep a record of the gifts you have received. Space has been provided for this purpose in Chapter 8. The system is very simple. Buy small numbered stickers (or buy blank stickers and number them yourself). Attach a numbered sticker to each gift as it arrives and then transfer the number and description of each gift to the list.

A word of advice: Keep up with your thank-you notes. Don't save them up till you have a "good block of time" or you will be totally overwhelmed. Write one whenever you have a moment and the sentiment will be fresher and more meaningful.

PRELIMINARY PATTERN SELECTION

Selecting china, crystal, and silver is fun, but it can be overwhelming. Take along your mother, a friend, your fiancé, and your own good taste, and remember that balance is the key. Two more ornate patterns should be balanced by a simpler one.

CHINA SELECTION

Manufacturer/Pattern _____

Description _____

Cost per Five-Piece Place Setting _____

Available at _____

Manufacturer/Pattern _____

Description _____

Cost per Five-Piece Place Setting _____

Available at _____

Manufacturer/Pattern _____

Description _____

Cost per Five-Piece Place Setting _____

Available at _____

Manufacturer/Pattern _____

Description _____

Cost per Five-Piece Place Setting _____

Available at _____

CRYSTAL/GLASSWARE SELECTION

Manufacturer/Pattern _____

Description _____

Price per Stem: Water_____Wine_____

Champagne _____Liquor_____

Available at _____

Manufacturer/Pattern _____

Description _____

Price per Stem: Water_____Wine_____

Champagne _____Liquor_____

Available at _____

Manufacturer/Pattern _____

Description _____

Price per Stem: Water_____Wine_____

Champagne _____Liquor_____

Available at _____

Manufacturer/Pattern _____

Description _____

Price per Stem: Water_____Wine_____

Champagne _____Liquor_____

Available at _____

FLATWARE SELECTION

Manufacturer/Pattern _____

Description _____

Price per Five-Piece Place Setting_____

Dinner Fork_____ Salad Fork_____

Dinner Knife _____ Teaspoon _____

Soup Spoon _____ Other_____

Available at _____

Manufacturer/Pattern _____

Description _____

Price per Five-Piece Place Setting_____

Dinner Fork_____ Salad Fork_____

Dinner Knife _____ Teaspoon _____

Soup Spoon _____ Other_____

Available at _____

Manufacturer/Pattern _____

Description _____

Price per Five-Piece Place Setting_____

Dinner Fork_____ Salad Fork_____

Dinner Knife _____ Teaspoon _____

Soup Spoon _____ Other_____

Available at _____

FINAL GIFT REGISTRY

Fine China

Manufacturer/Pattern _____

Piece(#) _____ Price _____

Registered at _____

Notes _____

_____

_____

Everyday China

Manufacturer/Pattern _____

Piece(#) _____ Price _____

Registered at _____

Notes _____

_____

_____

Silver Flatware

Manufacturer/Pattern _____

Piece(#) _____ Price _____

Registered at _____

Notes _____

_____

_____

_____

FINAL GIFT REGISTRY

Stainless Flatware

Manufacturer/Pattern _____

Piece(#) _____Price_____

Registered at _____

Notes _____

_____

_____

Crystal

Manufacturer/Pattern _____

Piece(#) _____Price_____

Registered at _____

Notes _____

_____

_____

Other Glassware and Crystal

Manufacturer/Pattern _____

Piece(#) _____Price_____

Registered at _____

Notes _____

_____

_____

_____

OTHER GIFTS REGISTERED BY STORE

Store _____

Address_____

Phone _____

Contact _____

Cookware   Price

_____   _____

_____   _____

_____   _____

_____   _____

Serving Pieces   Price

_____   _____

_____   _____

_____   _____

_____   _____

_____   _____

Bar Ware   Price

_____   _____

_____   _____

_____   _____

_____   _____

_____   _____

OTHER GIFTS REGISTERED BY STORE

Appliances   Price

_____   _____

_____   _____

_____   _____

_____   _____

_____   _____

_____   _____

Home Decor and Accessories   Price

_____   _____

_____   _____

_____   _____

_____   _____

_____   _____

Linens   Price

_____   _____

_____   _____

_____   _____

_____   _____

_____   _____

_____   _____

_____   _____

GIFTS FOR OTHERS

You will be receiving most of the presents, but there will undoubtedly be those people to whom you would like to give something as well. It is traditional to present your bridesmaids and maid of honor with a keepsake, and you might want to buy a special gift for your groom. There may be others you'd like to remember as well—friends who host parties or the aunt who performed airport duty.

For _Warren for Video tapping_

Gift _____ Price _____

Store _____ Phone _____

For _Andrey Keith (Soloist)_

Gift _____ Price _____

Store _____ Phone _____

For _____

Gift _____ Price _____

Store _____ Phone _____

For _____

Gift _____ Price _____

Store _____ Phone _____

For _____

Gift _____ Price _____

Store _____ Phone _____

For _____

Gift _____ Price _____

Store _____ Phone _____

GIFTS FOR OTHERS

For _____

Gift _____ Price _____

Store _____ Phone _____

For _____

Gift _____ Price _____

Store _____ Phone _____

For _____

Gift _____ Price _____

Store _____ Phone _____

For _____

Gift _____ Price _____

Store _____ Phone _____

CHARITABLE GIVING

Most weddings are celebrated with a certain extravagance and yours is probably no exception. But as you plan parties and select gifts, you may want to consider that for too many people the bare necessities are still out of reach. Some couples are finding that remembering those in need makes their wedding take on a deeper meaning.

You could simply make a donation to a favorite cause; consider giving a percentage of the total amount you will spend on the wedding reception. You might arrange to give left-overs from the reception to a local food bank that distributes to the homeless. Think about getting your guests involved; for instance, everyone could be asked to bring an article of old clothing. We've even heard of couples who ask that donations be made to a particular charity in lieu of conventional wedding gifts.

Whatever approach you take, a little imagination and compassion may make your wedding day special for others as well.

Chapter 10

Practical Matters

*T*he few months before a wedding are highly charged ones, emotional and exciting, but don't forget that there are some more mundane items that must be dealt with. After all, a wedding is a legal ceremony. You can't get married without blood tests and a marriage license, so be sure to investigate state requirements early. Remember, you must get your license in the state in which the wedding will take place. This might take as little as a day or as long as a week. If you and/or your fiancé live elsewhere, arrange to arrive in time to apply for and receive the license. (You must make application together.)

Are you planning to take your husband's name after the wedding? There are steps that should be taken now to minimize confusion later. Do you need a will? Are you and your fiancé interested in a prenuptial agreement? Must you change your home and health insurance policies? Do your honeymoon plans require a passport or visa? Do you know the deadline for submitting your wedding announcement to the newspapers?

All this may sound dull compared to picking out wedding dresses and flowers and champagne, but it is essential nonetheless. Attention to these details will insure that your marriage gets off to the right start after the wedding.

BLOOD TESTS

You will have to wait a few days to get the results, so be sure to schedule your appointment to get your marriage license accordingly.

Lab/Address _____

Phone _____

Hours _____Fee_____

Waiting Period _____Valid for_____

Appointment Scheduled _____

MARRIAGE LICENSE

Call well in advance to inquire about the necessary papers; requirements vary from state to state.

City Clerk Address_____

Phone_____Hours_____

Fee_____Valid for_____

Papers Needed:
    ☐ Birth Certificate
    ☐ Driver's License
    ☐ Blood Test
    ☐ Proof of Divorce
    ☐ Proof of Citizenship
Other_____

_____

_____

_____

Appointment Scheduled _____

_____

INSURANCE

Be certain that your family's homeowners insurance covers your wedding presents. You or your parents may need to add a floater policy.

Policy _____

Agent/Company _____

Phone _____

Payment Due _____

You and your husband-to-be should also investigate health insurance. If you both work, see which company offers the better package. If you are not yet working, make certain that you are put on your husband's policy, effective the date of the wedding. Once married, you will no longer be covered by your parents' policy. You will also need homeowners/renters insurance to cover your wedding gifts once they are in your new home. They are valuable.

Agent/Company _____

Address _____

Phone _____

Coverage _____

Payment Due _____

_____

Agent/Company _____

Address _____

Phone _____

Coverage _____

Payment Due _____

_____

CHANGING YOUR NAME

Investigate your state's policy on changing your name after marriage. Generally, if you wish to keep your name, you do nothing. If you wish to take your husband's name, you must make the appropriate changes promptly. Keep this checklist of officials and agencies who must be notified of your change in status.

☐ Social Security　　　　☐ Passport

☐ Motor Vehicle　　　　☐ Voter Registration

☐ Personnel　　　　　　☐ University

☐ Insurance Agent　　　☐ Bank

☐ Credit Card Companies

Other legal documents/agencies _____

_____

_____

_____

SEEING AN ATTORNEY

You may also want to schedule an appointment with an attorney. You and your husband might be considering a prenuptial agreement, or you might want to have a will drawn up. A good attorney can advise you about these and other matters.

Attorney _____

Address _____

Phone _____

Appointment Scheduled _____

Notes _____

NEWSPAPER ANNOUNCEMENTS

Many newspapers have special forms that you can just fill in with details about your wedding. If your paper does not provide these, simply read their standard announcements and use them as a guide to writing your own.

Newspaper _____

Address _____

Phone _____

Society Editor _____

Special Requirements (Photo size, double-spaced, etc.) _____

Date Due _____

THE WEDDING TRIP

Your travel agent may be handling the details, but keep important names, dates, and phone numbers handy.

Travel Agent _____ Phone _____

Transportation Reservations

Carrier _____ Phone _____

Carrier _____ Phone _____

Carrier _____ Phone _____

Date _____ Carrier/Number _____

Date _____ Carrier/Number _____

Date _____ Carrier/Number _____

Date _____ Carrier/Number _____

Date _____ Carrier/Number _____

Confirm by _____ Confirmed _____

Hotel Reservations

Hotel _____Dates_____

Contact_____Phone_____

Send Deposit by _____Deposit Sent_____

Hotel _____Dates_____

Contact_____Phone_____

Send Deposit by _____Deposit Sent_____

Hotel _____Dates_____

Contact_____Phone_____

Send Deposit by _____Deposit Sent_____

Hotel _____Dates_____

Contact_____Phone_____

Send Deposit by _____Deposit Sent_____

Necessary Papers

☐ Passport   ☐ Visa

☐ Marriage License   ☐ Traveler's Checks

Other_____

_____

_____

_____

_____

_____

_____

Recommended Reading _____

_____

_____

_____

Recommended Restaurants _____

_____

_____

_____

_____

_____

_____

_____

_____

_____

Recommended Sightseeing and Side Trips _____

_____

_____

_____

_____

_____

_____

_____

_____

Notes